Lessons My KIDS TAUGHT ME

VOLUME 02

A DEVOTIONAL FOR *Moms*
TOO BUSY FOR DEVOTIONALS

LIS BURNS

LESSONS MY KIDS TAUGHT ME: VOLUME 2

Copyright © 2017 by Lis Burns

ISBN-13: 978-0692973011
ISBN-10: 069297301X

Printed in the United States of America

Cover design by Gabe Reyes
Interior production by Jason Burns
Editing by Leigh DeVore
Author photo by Tina Sargeant

DEDICATION

*This book is dedicated to my husband Jason.
The way you effortlessly father our children inspires
and challenges me. Thanks for partnering and
putting up with me while we travel this crazy
journey of parenthood together.*

Table of CONTENTS

INTRODUCTION

Since writing the first volume of this series, a lot has changed. A lot of that change is simply because my children are growing and I, in turn, have to grow along with them. I no longer have any babies in diapers (you guys, it's *amazing!*). There are no pacifiers lurking in hidden corners of my purse. My counter is entirely devoid of bottles. I do, however, have a new set of experiences that I will share with you in the pages of this book. I'm suddenly dealing with things like school bullies and balancing my children's extracurricular activities.

One thing that has not changed in the midst of all of my children's growth, however, is that they are still some of God's greatest sources of instruction in my life. It never ceases to amaze me just how often in parenting that I find myself on the receiving end of teaching.

> *Busy Moms, take heart! You can still feel connected to God...*

Just like the first volume of *Lessons My Kids Taught Me*, I pray this book will be a tool for you. The idea is that you will be able to grab the book and go. You can have this book in your bag to read while waiting for karate or ballet lessons to get out. You can have a copy in your car to help you get through the dreaded carline (honestly, do not get me started on carline rule breakers – it's a thing). I've even heard from many of you that this book was the perfect read for your, ahem, morning potty time.

I get that. I love that. I wrote these books for the people who truly have no other alone time but that.

Busy Moms, take heart! You can still feel connected to God every day, even when you don't have a lot of time to dedicate to devotions. This is volume 2, friends – let's do it together!

Lessons My
KIDS TAUGHT ME
VOLUME 02

A DEVOTIONAL FOR *Moms*
TOO BUSY FOR DEVOTIONALS

Day 1:
WHAT IS REWARDED
WILL BE REPEATED

Around the time my daughter, Ella, turned 18 months, I decided our lives weren't chaotic enough and that what we really needed to add to our lives was a puppy. Dumbest decision ever. We already had three kids and a senior citizen dog. My husband, Jason, and I pastor a church. I try to write books. The kids want to eat three times a day. But yeah, it was a kind of magical moment when, on Christmas morning, Drake, the baby Boston Terrier, showed up at our door.

Drake was immediately adorable and delicious, but also completely and totally unruly. He saw the world, including my carpet, as his own personal patch of grass. Those who told me that I should get the younger dog because the older dog would train it were LIARS. The opposite seemed to happen, in fact. Winston, our beloved old man dog that never did anything bad began to regress.

It was around this time that we began to see the necessity of a dog trainer, so we went to the trusted authority for all such things: Craigslist. Yes, we did. Enter Gene, a 75-year-old man with a skull hood ornament on his truck, who liked to mail his information through the actual mail, and never gave us an email. Gene came over one evening and "trained" Drake by sitting in a chair and taking copious handwritten notes about his behavior. Gene concluded the night by telling us that Drake was really hyper and to call if we wanted him to take Drake to the dog park—for $50 per trip.

After that failed attempt at training, we went back to basics. I bought a good, old-fashioned bag of dog treats and began to reward Drake when he did his business outside. It slowly (seriously slowly) started to work. It brought to mind a saying I heard once that struck a chord with me:

What is rewarded will be repeated.

This is true in parenting, as well. It's so simple, and yet it always puzzles me how quick I am to jump to a negative exhortation before I celebrate something positive. But the truth is that my kids come alive when I praise them and encourage them.

And aren't I the same?

Don't I shine when I'm told I did well at something, and doesn't it make me want to repeat that and go even further the next time? Our kids need us to let them know when they've done good. When we shower them with the love and praise they so crave, we let them know that whatever it is that earned this reward is something they definitely can and should do again.

Today, instead of coming down on our kids for the things they're not doing right, let's celebrate them and the things they do get right each day. I truly believe we'll see that what is rewarded will become repeated.

Today's Scripture: **"The Lord rewards everyone for their righteousness and faithfulness" (1 Samuel 26:23 NIV).**

Today's Prayer: *Lord, thank You for showing me kindness. I pray that today I would do the same for my children. Let me be an earthly example of Your heavenly love today. I want to be gracious and encouraging to my kids, as You have been to me. Help me with that today, Lord. Amen.*

Day 2:
ACCIDENTALLY ON ACCIDENT

Middle children are fun, aren't they? I often marvel over my son Gavin and how he seems the least like me as a person. He's just his own cool, super-fun, always-up-for-a-good-time dude. I've also found that as the middle child he somehow seems to get mixed up in all the drama, whether it's as his older brother's scapegoat or his younger sister's chaperone. Poor guy has an alarming amount of confessional moments, it seems.

One such confession came on an otherwise normal afternoon. I was trying to accomplish something (note the key word *trying*) in another room, when a loud bang suddenly roared through the house. I sprinted toward the direction I'd heard the noise, only to be met with an extremely guilty-looking Gavin.

"Gavin! What happened?" I demanded as I did a quick check to ensure all his limbs were intact.

"Well, um…you see, I, um…" my poor boy stammered and began to wring his hands (never a good sign).

"Gavin, what happened!" I repeated, more forcefully this time.

"Well, I accidentally on accident may have accidentally had an accident. I'll fix it!"

The incident in question was, of course, the great Lego cyclone of 2016. I try not to think about that dark day too often, but, alas, we all fight our battles. In his bumbling attempt to explain what had happened, my poor Gavin had said the word *accident* or some other variation no less than four times. He wanted to make sure I knew that whatever had happened, he did *not* mean it. It was an accident.

I think a lot of us live our lives accidentally on accident. We stumble about, never taking responsibility for our actions, never becoming intentional about the things we do want. No, we simply treat life as one great accident.

Today, let's take a hold of our purpose! Let's own our past mistakes while not letting them define us. Let's be intentional about the work set before us. Let's endeavor to not just survive, but to thrive and do all the day's tasks with diligence and excellence! We can't do anything accidentally on accident, but we can do everything when we are in line with the God who has a purpose for us and is standing before us saying, "Come on! Let's do this!"

Today's Scripture: **"Do you see a man who excels in his work? He will stand before kings; he will not stand before unknown men" (Proverbs 22:29 NKJV).**

Today's Prayer: *Lord, I know that You have plans for me today. I don't want to walk around my life aimlessly. Instead, help me, today and every day, to execute my day with purpose and intentionality. I want to be someone who accomplishes all I can with Your help and guidance. Thank You for guiding my efforts. Amen.*

Day 3:
WHAT HAPPENED TO YOUR FAITH?

A few years ago, my oldest son, Joey, threw me into a faith crisis. We had been at a church service at my parent's church, and they were campaigning to raise money for a new building. As we were leaving the service, Joey came to me and said that he believed God had spoken to him to give all his money to that effort.

As a mom, my heart froze. I thought immediately of the neatly stacked bills that sat in his Lego wallet and how he had proudly saved birthday and lemonade stand money. There was a part of me that immediately wanted to tell him, "No, honey, that's OK. That's so sweet that you want to do that, but you don't have to."

> *God is still speaking to us now as much as He did when we were children, but are we listening?*

But a bigger part of me was convicted. I remember being Joey's age and doing similar things. I remember feeling those first pullings of the Holy Spirit and knowing that it was God Himself telling me to do something. As a young girl, it was so simple to me. I heard, and I did. Easy. As I grew older, doubt and cynicism crept in. I replaced my initial obedience to those urges with justifications, explanations, and judgments, and I watched as those inclinations became fewer and further between.

With that in mind, we supported Joey as he sent all his money ($177, basically a fortune to a 9-year-old) to his grandparents' building campaign. He cried when he first realized he was officially broke, so his dad and I held him and told him that we were so proud of him and that you can never out-give God. We assured him that what he had done by obeying God would never be wasted.

Watching Joey wrestle with his own understanding of what it meant to hear God was one of the biggest reality checks I've ever encountered in understanding my own obedience to His voice. What had happened to my own childlike trust? How many times has the Lord told me to do something BIG like He had told Joey, except instead of a young, receptive heart, it had fallen on jaded ears and a heart tampered by fear?

Let's find inspiration in the simplicity of Joey's obedience to God's gentle guiding. Maybe for a while now we've been ignoring special instructions that we need to pay more heed. God is still speaking to us now as much as He did when we were children, but are we listening? Do we brush off His leadings as the folly of our imaginations? Today, let's let faith lead and watch as God uses us in new ways!

Today's Scripture: **"Obey what I command you today" (Exodus 34:11a NIV).**

Today's Prayer: *Lord, please forgive me for allowing layers of callous to form over my heart for You. I want to listen and obey to every leading You give. I don't want to shut out the thoughts I determine couldn't possibly be from You. Help me to peel back the layers of my unbelief and find a new, childlike faith each and every day.*

Day 4:
BEWARE OF WHERE YOU FOCUS

In the summer of 2016, we moved into a new home. By all accounts this was an upward move. The house was larger, the boys no longer had to share a room, and we were closer to our church. However, this move also necessitated a change of schools for Joey and Gavin. We had all come to really love the school we were leaving, so this was not an easy transition. Joey had been there since kindergarten and Gavin since preschool.

The first few days, I joined the (inexplicably long) carline and eagerly awaited the time I could pick up the boys and hear all about their day. As soon as the van door slid open, though, I noticed a sad look on my older son's face. I immediately blurted out, "How was your day?" and he gave me the obligatory reply, "Good."

When I pressed him a little further, though, he began to tell me that there had been a few things that had gone wrong. Once the dam was broken on things he didn't enjoy, it gave way to a waterfall of sadness. He began to tell me everything this school did differently than his previous school and how he had preferred his last school so much. This was only a few days into school, mind you, but he had already decided that it was a place he didn't like.

It broke my heart as his mom, and I knew I needed to help him redirect his attitude before it grew even worse. The next day, I encouraged him to tell me three good things that had happened at school that day and three things he enjoyed about his new school. It was amazing to watch how quickly his whole attitude and demeanor changed when his focus shifted from the negative to the positive.

I do this all.the.time. I catch myself thinking about (see also: obsessing over) the negative things in my life, only to then be puzzled when I'm in a foul mood. When I only take a moment to shift focus and start over with an attitude of gratefulness, I watch my day turn around completely.

Today, we have a choice to help set the direction of the outcome of our attitude. If we focus on the negative, our day will have no choice but to follow that line of thinking. If we can choose gratefulness, though, and focus on all the gifts we have in front of us, we'll also get an attitude adjustment for the better!

Today's Scripture: **"Remember the wonders he has done, his miracles, and the judgments he pronounced" (Psalm 105:5 NIV).**

Today's Prayer: *Lord, forgive me for having a negative focus. I choose today to begin to replace my grumbling with gratefulness. You have blessed me with so much, and I am truly thankful for each day I get to live on this Earth.*

Day 5:
DELAY TACTICS

My son Gavin suffers from what I call "procrastination syndrome." He will do anything at night to try and delay his bed time. He'll offer foot massages, give 10-minute-long hugs, etc. It's cute for the first few minutes, and then it just becomes tiresome. "Gavin, go to bed!" I'll say. He'll pull out his puppiest of puppy dog eyes, lashes all aflutter, and say something heart-melting along the lines of, "But I just love spending time with you!"

Interesting how he had all day to spend time with me, but only really seems to get into the idea when it's his bedtime. *Hmm.*

I can only get irritated to a limited extent with Gavin when it comes to his nightly delay tactics, though. Why? Because I'm just like him when it comes to doing the things I know I'm supposed to do. Ouch.

Why do we come up with every excuse in the book to delay doing what we know we need to do or can do? We let fear, self-doubt, laziness and pride stand in the way of our destiny, so convinced by our own excuses that we truly believe we're doing the right thing.

Denial can be a powerful thing. Particularly when we use it in God's name. What do I mean? You can use even the most holy of reasons to delay going after something you are called to do: *I don't think this is of God because it makes me too uncomfortable when I think about it* (side note: God's call has never been about our own comfort), or *I'm too busy serving in the last assignment God gave me to do, so I can't do that right now.*

Go after your dreams. At all costs. God has placed those dreams within you for a reason, and they will not get done if you start to self-sabotage by employing every little-known delay tactic in the book.

Let's not be like Gavin at bedtime. Let's accept what we have to do and live with passion for that purpose at the forefront of our hearts and minds. Sometimes the only thing stopping us is us!

Go after your dreams. At all costs.

Today's Scripture: **The Parable of the Great Banquet, Luke 14:15–24**

Today's Prayer: *Lord, forgive me for making excuses. I have heard Your voice calling to me, and I will listen. I want to stop letting fear or doubt disguise itself as a legitimate reason to keep disobeying You.*

Day 6:
DADDY, I'M BEAUTIFUL!

After years of knowing only the joys of boy parenting, having Ella brought such new insight into our world. One of the many ways she is different from the boys is her instant and innate love for all things dressy. She loves shoes, she loves (pretend) makeup, and she loves to twirl in a princess dress.

Shortly after Ella turned 2, I began noticing a trend in our morning dress up routine. After helping her into whatever colorful frock she chose for the day, without thinking I would always say: "Oh, Ella, you're so beautiful! Go show your daddy how beautiful you are!"

In an instant, she was off, running down the hall screaming: DADDY! I'M BEAUTIFUL!

After a week or two of this, I no longer had to tell her to go show her daddy. She'd simply wait until her final touches were complete, and then take off, running at full-speed to go show Jason her outfit of the day. Her excitement to show her father her beauty made me think about how I interact with my heavenly Father.

We show God that we're beautiful not when we wear a princess dress, but when we come before Him, fully forgiven and free. We can cry at Him with assurance, "Daddy, I'm beautiful!" and it's true because He made us that way.

Somewhere along the way, it became a trend that NOT knowing you are beautiful was a beautiful or desired attribute in a woman. I get the idea behind it: no one likes people who are full of themselves. But there's a big difference between knowing you are beautiful and lording that over others.

Knowing we are beautiful and that our "Daddy" cannot wait to watch us shine is something we should all work on. Let's take a lesson from Ella. Today, let's proudly come before Him, confident in His love and grace, eager to show Him and the world that we are His beautiful daughters. If Jason can't wait to see Ella's pretty dresses each day, how much more must our very Creator delight in seeing us run to Him to show Him that we are beautiful in freedom and confidence.

Let's take a page out of Ella's book today and run to our Father with full confidence that He can't wait to see us. He thinks we're beautiful.

Today's Scripture: **"The LORD delights in those who fear him, who put their hope in his unfailing love" (Psalm 147:11 NIV).**

Today's Prayer: *Lord, sometimes I don't feel beautiful, but I know You see me that way. Help my unbelief. May Your confidence and belief in me encourage my own belief. Thank You for not caring about the things that this world sees and for truly valuing my heart. You see and You know, and I love that about You. Thank You, Father!*

Day 7:
FIX YOUR OWN ROOM

My oldest son is so much like me sometimes. This can be really fun and great (like when he shares my love for super-random humor) or horrifying and convicting (like when I watch him stress over perfectionism). One way in which we're very similar is our absolute obsession with cleanliness. I like things neat and tidy, and he is just the same. Joey's room is, on any given day, always perfectly clean and organized. That's my boy!

One day, while at a friend's house, Joey disappeared for a few minutes. I didn't think anything of it as he returned soon enough. Later that evening, however, I received a text message from my friend.

"So, Joey made Jack's bed and left this."

Along with the text was a picture of a note Joey had written and left on the bed that he had, in fact, made. It said: "Dear Jack, I made your bed. Love, Joey."

I was a little bit embarrassed and a little bit proud.

Joey's love for the orderly had probably gone too far. It's not his responsibility to make other people's beds. It's not his job to assess how good of a job his buddy is doing on room cleanliness. He is only responsible for his own room. That's it.

It's the same for us. We can't look at those around us and try to assess how good or bad we think they're doing. At the end of the day, we're responsible only for our own actions. We can't control the actions of others. We can get so focused on the wrongs of our neighbors that we forget the problems in our own lives that we need to fix!

Joey needs to worry only about his own room. In the same way, you and I need to focus on only our own hearts and actions. When our main focus and obsession becomes how well (or not well) someone else is living, we miss the point and begin to lose sight of our own faults. Let's not judge others while ignoring our own flaws. Let's fix our own rooms and leave the rest to God's care!

Today's Scripture: **"How can you say to your brother, 'Let me remove the speck from your eye'; and look, a plank is in your own eye?" (Matthew 7:4 NKJV).**

Today's Prayer: *Lord, forgive me for wasting energy on worry for the actions of others, while I still have so much to fix in my own life and heart. I want to be all I can be in You today, and I can't do that if my focus is on other people and their flaws. Thank You for allowing me to see the areas of myself that need fixing. I know that with Your help I can make the changes I need to make. Amen.*

Day 8:
UNEXPECTED BESTIES

We have very similar brown eyes. She is loud, and so am I. We both laugh with our entire being. We're both embarrassingly addicted to popcorn. Shoes are a weakness for both of us; we never feel like our outfits are complete without the right pair to match.

We have so much in common, despite our substantial age gap. You might think it strange to hear that one of my dearest friends is 32 years younger, but, hey, what can I say? She had me with a first glance at those brown eyes. My bestie? The one I laugh with daily? The girl who has my whole heart? She's only 3 years old. She's my daughter, Ella.

Ella is possibly the most intimidating person I've ever encountered. Yes, I once provided myself to her as a literal body B and B, but from the moment that ultrasound tech said the words, "It's a girl," I was flat-out scared.

Why?

> *Your bestie may wind up coming from a place you least expected.*

Girls are emotional (I'm emotional). Girls are unpredictable (I'm unpredictable). Girls can judge other girls in ways we never judge our male counterparts (I'm pleading the fifth here).

At the end of the day, though, I knew all of those objections to having a daughter were mere masks for my deeper fear: I worried I wasn't ready to be a role model for a girl who would look to me for guidance and example.

Having a daughter brought out some of my deepest insecurities and fears. But from the first day all 9 pounds of her were placed in my exhausted arms, I've been in love with Ella. I realized that on the other side of my fears lay some of the greatest connections and love I've ever experienced.

Ella is my bestie. She's my shopping buddy, my cuddle partner, and the one I want to grab for a fun girl's day out. What we lack in common ground of life experience, we make up for in understanding and soul connection. My daughter is the friend who was chosen for me. You've heard of making friends? I literally *made* Ella. That's beautiful and humbling and amazing.

Besties don't have to look like you, like the things you like, or have gone to high school at the same time you did. Your bestie may wind up coming from a place you least expected. If we limit ourselves to a pool of bestie candidates that mirror only our own reflections, we may be missing out on the privilege of finding a new lifelong friend. Let's broaden our scope today and discover the joy of unexpected besties!

Today's Scripture: **"A friend loves at all times" (Proverbs 17:17a NIV).**

Today's Prayer: *Lord, thank You for those who think and act and look differently than me. I ask that You would open my eyes to all that they can teach me today. Help me to not close myself off when I get scared, but to embrace the new and beautiful things You are bringing my way. Amen.*

Day 9:
THE GIFT OF TIME

One morning I was in "go" mode. I was checking things off my to-do list at an admirable rate, and I had the day ahead planned down to the minute in order to finish the rest of said list. I had moved to another part of the house to try to get some studying and writing done, when suddenly my daughter, Ella, burst into tears and undecipherable grunts.

I'll sheepishly admit that my first thought may have been, "Ugh, my to-do list was going so well." But I quickly looked down at her fat tears and scooped her up. "What's wrong, baby?"

"Iadfwannafadkplayakdfjwithafdyou."

"What?"

"I wanna play with you."

Oh…Her need wasn't something I could throw a quick fix on. She wanted the one thing that I was needing the most for myself in that moment: my time. Didn't she know that my busyness often was because I was trying to do things to make her life better? Or that I was often so busy because I wanted to make her proud of me? But to a 2-year-old child, none of that really matters. What she wanted was just to play with me. She wanted me. Just me.

I can get so busy doing things *for* my kids that I forget to simply *be* with them. And aren't we the same with God? I'm so guilty of this as someone in ministry. I fill my calendar with things (good things, even) *for* God, but when was the last time I simply sat to *be* with Him?

Lists and planning are good, but we have to always be ready to push those aside at a moment's notice when there is something that matters more. If I'm so caught up in making sure a list gets done that I miss the beautiful moments that God has for me, what's the good of my list?

Today, let's not miss life. The things I look back on and remember are not the minor daily accomplishments, but the moments of my daughter's laughter or the times when I met a friend's need because I was obedient to God's prompts. He is speaking, if we'll just listen.

Today's Scripture: "**As Jesus and his disciples were on their way, he came to a village where a woman named Martha opened her home to him. She had a sister called Mary, who sat at the Lord's feet listening to what he said. But Martha was distracted by all the preparations that had to be made. She came to him and asked, 'Lord, don't you care that my sister has left me to do the work by myself? Tell her to help me!' 'Martha, Martha,' the Lord answered, 'you are worried and upset about many things, but few things are needed — or indeed only one. Mary has chosen what is better, and it will not be taken away from her'" (Luke 10:38–42 NIV).**

Today's Prayer: *Lord, forgive me for my obsession with busy. I want to be with You more than I want to cross any one item off a to-do list. Here am I, ready and willing to meet with You. I ask that You'd speak because I am listening. Now, today, and always. Amen.*

Day 10:
CALL IT WHAT IT IS

There are certain conversations that I just adore having with my kids. I love talking about their days, hearing them tell me the different ways they experience God, or listening to them recount something that made them laugh. There are other conversations, however, that I positively dread having with them.

One completely insignificant Monday, my son Joey came home from fourth grade and told me in his own vernacular that he had encountered racism for the first time. He had watched as two boys in his class made disparaging remarks about another girl based solely on the color of her skin.

My soul was crushed to hear this. It's hard to watch as your children realize the world isn't quite as pure as they originally imagined. Still, these conversations are important, so I knew I had to use this moment to explore and teach. I asked Joey what he thought about the situation, and he seemed genuinely confused that they would be making assumptions about the girl based purely on her skin color. I asked him what he did in response. He said he simply turned to the boys and asked:

"Are you making fun of her?"

I'll admit, at first, I wished he had said more. I wanted to hear him say that he'd jumped up in indignation and screamed, "NO!" I wanted to hear him be a champion of those oppressed by injustice. But the more I thought about it, the more I began to realize that his reply was kind of perfect.

Why?

Because he was simply calling this thing what it was. That's important.

We like to hide behind terms and phrases and defend our actions with justifications hidden behind better intentions. The truth is, though, that things just are what they are. Maybe some of us have been justifying our behaviors behind fancy words and layers of denial, but it's time to become like children again and take truly honest looks at our hearts.

Let's peel away the layers of cynicism and indifference that are clouding our assessments today and get simple. Sin is simply sin. We can call is many different things, but at the root of it is the same evil. On a positive note, no sin is so great that it can't be as simply repented of and redeemed from in a simple act of repentance.

Today's Scripture: **"Let the one who does wrong continue to do wrong; let the vile person continue to be vile; let the one who does right continue to do right; and let the holy person continue to be holy" (Revelation 22:11 NIV).**

Today's Prayer: *Lord, forgive me for trying to spin my sin into anything other than an affront to You and Your goodness. I repent of my wrongs, and I thank You that You will help me overcome all things. Today, I want to simplify my view, and I know You can help me to do that through Your Holy Spirit. Amen.*

Day 11:
I TAUGHT MY KIDS EVERYTHING BUT THE MOST IMPORTANT THING

One Sunday morning, we were driving to church, and I casually threw out a reference to something in my past without thinking. My younger son spoke up from the backseat with a crinkled nose: "What do you mean?" he asked. I chuckled and rolled my eyes and asked his older brother to tell him about it. Older brother just gave me a blank look.

I started to get concerned.

"Surely, I've told you that story before?" I asked, trying to keep the panic out of my voice.

All I got in return were two shaking heads and an inquiry for me to please tell them.

I was floored. In all my mom-ing, I try to incorporate a deep understanding that God is everything to us and so inextricably interwoven into the fabric of who we are. I have told them about my own healing from cancer and how good God has been to me. But I need to tell them more. The story in question was one that was so huge in my own timeline that I just assumed that two of the most important people in my life would obviously know all about it. But they didn't. Because I hadn't told them.

I want my stories of faith to become part of their heritage and legacy until they can give my testimony better than me. Why? Because it matters. Without God's faithfulness, these beautiful babies wouldn't even be here. It's important that they know where they came from. In fact, it's downright biblical.

The people of Israel had seen God do some amazing things. This is an understatement, so let me rephrase that. The people of Israel saw food drop from the sky, a sea split in half, and a cloud of fire. Their minds had been blown by God's greatness. Sadly, though, when the older generation of Israel began to die, and the people were firmly settled in their promised land, the memories of God's provision also began to fade with the rising of the new generation.

The stories that they no longer knew had once been the most important thing to their elders. These miracles were as integral to their story as their very names. And yet, mere years later, their children and grandchildren didn't even know that they had occurred, nor the God who had brought them to pass. This is a total and complete travesty.

Let's not be like the people described in Judges. We have to tell our children about God's faithfulness to us. If not, we risk a rising generation who has no idea of the impact that God has had upon us and why it is part of the very foundation of who we are. In all our teaching, let's remember to tell the stories of God's miracles so that our children live on in their power and impact for generations to come.

Today's Scripture: **"After that whole generation had been gathered to their ancestors, another generation grew up who knew neither the LORD nor what he had done for Israel" (Judges 2:10 NIV).**

Today's Prayer: *Lord, forgive me for failing to pass on Your greatness and goodness. May I always remember to tell the stories of Your faithfulness to me and the generations before me. You have been good, Lord, and I want to tell my children about You and all You've been to me.*

Day 12:
SCHOOL SUPPLY SADNESS

It all started with a simple, innocuous email. ORDER YOUR SCHOOL SUPPLIES FOR NEXT YEAR, it said. I was cool with that. I'm a planner to the very core and anything that lessens my to-do list is a thing of joy and beauty.

I was doing fine and dandy, perusing the site and entering the appropriate info. Until all the sudden, something awful happened.

Enter your child's grade for NEXT YEAR, it said. Suddenly, I paused. I clicked on the drop-down box and had to double take three times before realizing my oldest son was entering his final year of elementary school. By this time next year, I realized, he'd be in middle school.

My heart sank to the gray wooden floor of my kitchen.

How and when and why had this happened? How could it be that my oldest son was only going to have one more year of elementary school? How could I be the mom of an almost middle school student? I was not ready for middle school! Middle school was full of hormones and drama and boys with facial hair! My Joey was a baby! A BABY! I was not ready to admit that he had been doing a lot of growing while I was busy with life.

Oh, my heart. I remember wishing away the baby days with all my might. It's hard. Not sleeping, no time for yourself, and little people who depend on you for absolutely everything. Yet, even in all the craziness of that life, it was beautiful. Now, as I sat at my kitchen counter crying over file folders and pencil purchases, it hit me just how fast this parenting thing was going.

Parenting is filled with long days and short years. I once heard this phrase, and it absolutely kicked me in the gut with its accuracy. I've caught myself wishing the days of infancy away in exchange for the greener pastures of older childhood, only to arrive there and realize I miss those early moments so much.

The truth is that every single day is precious and has to be treated as such. We can't wait for things to come, or we'll miss life in the present. This life is fast, and nothing makes us realize just how fast like the growth of our kids. If we are faithful to remain present and not try to get too far ahead of current reality, we'll find that the school supply purchases won't hit us quite so hard.

Today's Scripture: **"Why, you do not even know what will happen tomorrow. What is your life? You are a mist that appears for a little while and then vanishes" (James 4:14 NIV).**

Today's Prayer: *Lord, thank You for every moment of life with my babies. It's going fast, but I recognize that You are the giver of every single breath. Help me to relax more, even as I am tempted to entertain discontentedness. I want to live today to the fullest. I want to look back on my children's lives with fondness that we spent every moment well. Thank you for a new start each day to embrace this life You've given me.*

Day 13:
GOOD DIFFERENT

It was 2015 when I finally gave in and witnessed a great death. The death was that of any of my possible remaining street cred. Cause of death? We bought a minivan. If I'm honest, though, it wasn't long before I was truly in love with Van-essa. (Listen, if you've already acknowledged that you are no longer cool, you may as well go all the way.) This van carries my family of five with ease and room to spare. The DVD player that I swore we'd never use unless we were driving for distances of more than an hour away (snort) has soothed my crying baby so I could get calls done. It's the most comfortable vehicle ever. Truly, I love her.

More than anything, I appreciate the van for its practicality. Around the time my daughter came of preschool age, I realized that each of my three children now had weekly activities to attend. There was piano for the boys, dance for Ella, extra rehearsals for the school musical for Joey, and soccer for Gavin. The van had quite literally become a taxi, catering to the ever-increasing demands of my kids' schedules.

Realizing how many activities we were involved in made me realize that my kids are so, so different and, as such, are all gifted in different ways.

This matters because I can't expect my kids to be interested in the same activities. Nor, if I'm smart, do I want them to all do the same activities. Gavin is pretty good at soccer, and his older brother is an incredible public speaker. I want to put them into things that help foster the gifts they've been given instead of wishing them into abilities they don't have.

That didn't stop them from having feelings of jealousy as they watched their sibling excel in something that they weren't a part of, though. Joey may have looked on wistfully as Gavin received a soccer award, or Gavin may have gotten extra quiet during Joey's speech competition weekends. But for the sake of time and wisdom, I had made a decision to only invest in the things they showed a propensity toward. I simply don't have time or energy to do all the things for all the kids.

It's quite the same for me. I look around at others and I'm tempted to want the gifts they have. I wish I was an amazing chef like Susan or that I excelled in exercise like Deb. But the simple fact is that I'm not Susan or Deb. They have gifts that I don't, and, incidentally, I have gifts that they don't. Wanting to be more like someone else or to do something I haven't been blessed with the ability to do is pointless and being ungrateful. Instead of wasting energy wanting to be someone else, how about investing more energy into being the best Lis that I can be?

We have to stop the comparison trap. Different is good and necessary. We were all made with specific roles to play. If we are too busy wishing for another part, our parts are being left undone. The world can't afford to not have us in our spots! We are important! We are needed!

Today's Scripture: **"For just as each of us has one body with many members, and these members do not all have the same function, so in Christ we, though many, form one body, and each member belongs to all the others"** (Romans 12:4–5 NIV).

Today's Prayer: *Lord, forgive me for wishing away the things that You've blessed me with. I'm so grateful to be able to play any part in Your great story. Make me forever aware of what I can do to bring Your love to this world. Amen.*

Day 14:
I STILL LOVE YOU THE SAME

My children are so incredibly classic when it comes to personality characteristics based on birth order. My oldest son is a rule follower, a neatnik, and an overachiever. My middle son is care-free and the life of the party. And my baby girl is the very definition of a baby sister (please send prayers and sparkly things).

I love that Joey wants to do well in school. I love his determination and work ethic. I don't love, however, when he breaks down in tears because he's stressed over an assignment or worried he didn't get a 100 percent on a test.

One day, I called Joey into my room and had him sit on my bed. I asked him what he thought would happen if he didn't get all A's? His eyes grew wide. To him, that was unthinkable. He wanted all A's. He assumed I wanted him to get all A's. And I do, if that's something he is capable of doing. But what I don't want is a son who works himself so hard that he doesn't enjoy school or learning or life.

I explained to Joey that whether he got A's, B's, or C's, I'd still love him just the same. I told him that, as his mom, my heart is so much more concerned with who he is than with what he can do. My love for him is not based on his performance.

Oh, how my gut clenches even writing that.

I am so much like Joey when it comes to my relationship with God. I want to earn things such as love, approval and favor. That's so laughable. But I still try! Somehow, I think I am so accustomed to the earthly scales of a "What can you do for me?" mentality, that I figure God surely must view me the same. I picture God keeping some sort of record book of my deeds that He uses to dole out grace. Oh, what a lie!

> *The sooner we can understand and accept the gifts of God, the sooner we can find freedom in Him.*

Joey can't earn my love. I simply love him. If he gets A's, I may celebrate his accomplishment, but my love remains as steadfast and as true as it always was. God sees us, His children, just the same. He loves us. Period. If we have a great week or if we mess up, His love remains unchanged. Similarly, we can't earn His gifts. He gives them freely and without performance-based ratings.

The sooner we can understand and accept the gifts of God, the sooner we can find freedom in Him. Let's start retraining our brains to think of God as a GIVER of good gifts and not a score-keeper. When we accept the gift of His love and grace, we'll find that we are more graceful and loving to those around us, as well.

Today's Scripture: **"For it is by grace you have been saved, through faith — and this is not from yourselves, it is the gift of God" (Ephesians 2:8 NIV).**

Today's Prayer: *Thank You, Lord, for the FREE gifts of Your mercy and grace. I am forever humbled by these gifts that I can do nothing to earn. Today, I repent of my attempts to try to deserve them. May I walk in the confidence and knowledge that You love me unconditionally. Amen.*

Day 15:
THANKFUL FOR ME

Having two sons and then a daughter, I was truly unprepared for the whirlwind that is my darling Ella. She blew away all my previous knowledge of what being a mom meant, and she challenged my expectation on every level. This girl is fierce and strong and sassy, while simultaneously remaining the sweetest little love you've ever met.

When she was around 2 years old, my husband and I began to notice a fairly comedic trend in her evening prayers. We'd give her a bath, brush her teeth, read her a story, and then walk her through bedtime prayers. We'd ask her to repeat after us and say things such as "Thanks for a great day." We always ended the prayer by asking God to bless our family.

"Thank You, God, for Mommy and Daddy." She'd repeat.

"Thank You, God, for Joey and Gavin." She'd repeat.

"Thank You, God, for our dog Winston." She'd repeat.

"In Jesus' name…"

"And Ella!" she'd add heartily, before adding her own amen.

The first time she did it, we almost fell over laughing so hard. This girl was determined to thank God for herself. Herself. She would not let a prayer go by without inserting her own thanks for herself. Goodness, I love this child. My husband and I started adding prayers of thanks for ourselves to our prayer times and got quite the kick out of it.

Ella had no idea what she was doing or why it was funny. She simply wanted to be part of the prayer, and when she heard her family being listed, she wanted to be included in that list!

I laugh, but when I think about it, am I grateful for myself? My life is a gift, and I may often thank God for things He has given me, but what about just thanking God for me? He is the reason I have breath to breathe. He is the reason my heart is beating inside my body right now. He is everything. Should I not thank Him for that?

Let's take the truth from Ella's childlike prayer. Let's be thankful for our very being. Let's not just thank God for the things *in* our lives, but *for* our lives! We are here because of His design and purpose, and that's not something to take lightly! The same God who carved out the universe also saw fit to create us. That's pretty incredible!

Today, let's thank God for ourselves.

Today's Scripture: **"Rather, he himself gives everyone life and breath and everything else" (Acts 17:25b NIV).**

Today's Prayer: *Thank You, Father, for my life. I am grateful to be here on this Earth. I acknowledge that You are the reason I have life and breath and everything else. You are My Creator, and I'm grateful for me today. Amen.*

Day 16:
HERE I AM!

It was the actual cutest thing in the world to watch Ella discover how to play hide-and-go-seek. She loved the thrill and anticipation of counting to 10 (very, *very* slowly) and then running off to find her daddy or me. Her squeals and giggles when she found us would melt the most frozen of hearts. When it was her turn to hide, however, her performance was a little less than stellar.

The first time we played, she would go to the same exact hiding spot every.single.time: the bathtub. To add to the non-mystique, as we would walk around with exaggerated cries of "Where's Ella? Where could she be?" she'd actually shout out to us from the tub, "Here I am! I'm in here! I'm in the bathtub!"

> *Let's choose to speak life instead of death.*

This game quickly became a favorite pastime for my husband and me because it was just too adorable. Ella was completely missing the point of the game, and she could not have cared less. She was so thrilled to be playing a game with her parents, and her joy simply would not allow her to stay quiet.

I think a lot of us act like Ella playing hide-and-go-seek when it comes to allowing ourselves to be targeted by the enemy. Ouch. We go around shouting about our perceived weaknesses and inadequacies, essentially inviting him to attack us in our most vulnerable spots. He is looking for places to get a foot in the door where our souls are concerned, and a lot of us are (knowingly or not) all too willing to advertise just what we think we fail in.

Do we constantly talk about our hatred of our own bodies? Do we often mention how we aren't smart or qualified enough for a certain position? What about when we simply talk down about our abilities? When we do these things, we're waving a red flag of vulnerability, announcing that these are struggle areas and, as such, places where we can be attacked successfully.

Let's not shout out our hiding places, so-to-speak. Let's choose to speak life instead of death. Let's not make ourselves easy targets where the enemy is concerned. Instead, let's trust God's ability to "hide" our imperfections with His grace. He is more than enough where we lack. We don't have to walk around in defeat. We can embrace God's perfection for our imperfection, today and always.

Today's Scripture: **"Be alert and of sober mind. Your enemy the devil prowls around like a roaring lion looking for someone to devour" (1 Peter 5:8 NIV).**

Today's Prayer: *Lord, help me to speak life over myself. I ask forgiveness for announcing what I think are my weaknesses to the world and to the enemy. I repent for feeling inadequate, and I trust You to be more than enough for me. Thank You that You cover and protect me from the enemy's attacks. Amen.*

Day 17:
BACKING DOWN

I love my middle child. Obviously, I love all my children, but my middle child is so chill and easygoing and fun-loving. He's just a joy. He can age up and play with his older brother, or he can be a patient saint while playing with his little sister. Gavin is just a cool kid.

I remember going to his first-grade parent-teacher conference and sitting across from his darling of a teacher. She was full of praise for Gavin, and I was bursting at the seams hearing about him. Halfway through the meeting, though, she told me something that threw me for a loop.

"Gavin backs down from a challenge," she said. "Unless it's important to him."

My immediate thought was one of defense. I didn't like that my son would back down from confrontation or challenge. I am a bold personality, and I never shrink away from hard things. I worried that this character quality made my son somehow weak or less of a leader.

I soon realized, though, that Gavin's ability to sort out the important challenges from the less important ones was actually something I really love about him. Gavin is everyone's friend and hugely popular in his class. As I thought about him, I realized that his backing down in areas that others refused to probably created a healthy and peaceful environment in his classroom. I imagined all the fights that were prevented and the drama that was avoided because my son backed down on the lesser things.

The more I thought about it, the more I started to feel personally convicted by those words. Maybe it wasn't that Gavin needed to step up to more challenges, but maybe I needed to back down from more and wait until things were very important to me. I can be super confrontational, but if I'm honest, my combative nature has landed me in a lot more conflicts than I'd like to admit. That's not a great thing. Far from it, in fact.

Not everything is important. More "challenges" in our lives need to be backed down from in order to keep peace. The older I get, the more I realize that peace is so much of a greater goal than being right or winning. Not everything has to be a battle.

We can learn from Gavin today. Not every challenge needs our effort or energy. Sometimes, when it's important, we can rise up and meet those challenges. Other times, we can simply back down and count the costs. I think we'll find that when we do, our lives will be more peaceful and others will appreciate our ability to find wisdom in those decisions, as well.

Today's Scripture: **"Make every effort to keep the unity of the Spirit through the bond of peace" (Ephesians 4:3 NIV).**

Today's Prayer: *Lord, help me to discern when I need to fight and when I need to bite my tongue. I don't want to be combative just for the sake of the fight. I want to fight when it's important and worthy. Thank You for helping me know that difference today. Amen.*

Day 18:
TINY MIRRORS

I am an early riser. My daughter, Ella, is an (even earlier) early riser. I am a perfectionist. My son Joey is a perfectionist. I adore random humor. My son Gavin is the king of random humor. In varying degrees and in varying capacities my children all have parts of me within their own unique personalities. It's as fun and fascinating as it is scary and convicting.

What's hard is that I often get angry at my kids for things they do that are totally and completely things that I also do. My daughter busts into our room at 6:30 almost every morning. I get so annoyed until my husband looks at me and says, "Your daughter." Yes, she got that from me.

When my son Joey is being super hard on himself, I get frustrated with his inability to see how incredible he is. Then I remember that I struggle with never feeling quite enough, and I soften toward his struggle as I see my own reflection in it.

When Gavin is laughing so hard and so uncontrollably that he can't focus and becomes borderline annoying, I remember times when I would annoy my husband with my inability to focus for my belly-shaking laughter.

My kids will reflect what they see in me, but who am I reflecting? There are many times when I'm a wonderful example of things that I desperately want them to grasp in their own lives. Other times, though, I'm a person I would shudder to see reflected in them.

One day while coming upon a four-way stop, I started grumbling and shouting at a man in the lane over who completely ignored the stop sign and blew right through the intersection. When one of my children piped in with their own annoyance at the situation in a terse voice, I felt immediately ashamed of my actions. Children are tiny mirrors.

I don't have to (nor could I ever) be perfect. I can, however, invite God into my life and ask Him to take over where my flesh would want to surface. When God is in my day, I have a far better shot at reflecting His light and love for my children to see. Then I can rest assured knowing that when they inevitably start mirroring me, it will be something good and pure that they reproduce.

My kids will reflect what they see in me, but who am I reflecting?

Let's be sure today that we are acting as reflections of God's love. Our kids are not the only ones watching. We are to be a light to the whole world so that by our attitudes and actions we can show just how great our God is. Let's let God's love shine!

Today's Scripture: **"In the same way, let your light shine before others, that they may see your good deeds and glorify your Father in heaven" (Matthew 5:16 NIV).**

Today's Prayer: *Lord, forgive me for the times I've allowed my flesh to shine more than Your presence. I want to be a reflection of You so that others may see You in me. Thank You for grace as I endeavor to allow You free reign in my day. Amen.*

Day 19:
I HAVE TO GO!

I'm sure I can come across as a little emotionally volatile, and I won't deny that fact. But the truth is that having kids opens me up to being more emotionally vulnerable. As you read this, you can nod and agree that having a piece of you out there in the world is the most humbling, exhilarating and soul-changing thing you've ever done.

One recent excursion with intense emotion came as I was buying my daughter her first-ever backpack. Sure, she was only starting two-day-a-week preschool, and sure, even then, it was only for four hours at a time. But oh, my heart! My baby! My girl! How in the world could she already be going to school? How could she be leaving me and eating lunch without me and playing with others without me there to make sure she's OK?

As I began to tear up, I looked at her and said, "Ella, you just can't go to school!"

She looked at me, devoid of any emotional manipulation, and simply said: "I have to go."

Oof. My poor heart could barely handle it. She meant no harm, but she simply didn't understand the emotional ramifications that her going to school meant for me. It wasn't so much about the days or hours themselves, but rather the reminder that she was growing up without my permission.

Her response was completely normal and a lot more logical than mine. Ella knew she was now 3 and that we had decided she would start preschool at 3. She knew it was time to go, so she was ready to go. Period.

Lessons, lessons, lessons. I can learn so much from her lack of emotional response. Oh, how I let the things of this world entangle and ensnare me, keeping me from doing the things I know I have to do. I let emotions steer my decisions when they have no place being in the driver's seat. I need to learn from Ella and view situations on a truth-based reality only, denying hindering emotions the chance to slow my progress.

Today, we have to let our decisions and actions be guided solely by what we know to be God's truth. Emotions are amazing, but they have to stay in their place. Emotions should support the things we already know, as opposed to informing our actions against the truth. Let's remember to give emotions their space and nothing more. When we do, we'll find we can face any situation with a level head and a clear view of things. Why? Because, like Ella, we have to!

Today's Scripture: **"'Then you will know the truth, and the truth will set you free'" (John 8:32 NIV).**

Today's Prayer: *Lord, I am guilty of allowing my emotions to hinder my life. I don't want to be held back by things that I feel. Feelings are important, but they are not the ultimate truth. You are the truth. Help my actions to always reflect my belief in that. Amen.*

Day 20:
WHAT'S AFTER BREAKFAST?

Over the years, I've heard from several mom friends of mine who struggle with kids who are picky eaters. They tell me that it is the absolute worst having to argue and plead with their kids each night to please, *please*, PLEASE just eat something! While I certainly sympathize with their struggle, I in *no* way can relate to it. I gave birth to three of the world's heartiest eaters.

My kids love to eat so much, in fact, that they are all constantly asking me seemingly endless questions about when their next opportunity for food is. Ella will lay in bed after her nightly prayers and start asking me if she can have banana bread for breakfast the next morning. Gavin will finish his breakfast and ask me what's for dinner that night. Joey is famous for writing down on my shopping list all the foods he wants me to pick up at the grocery store. Food is a very important thing around the Burns household.

I'm guilty of the same food anxiety as my kids. I can be tempted to start worrying over dinner while I'm sipping my early-morning coffee. I look at upcoming food festivals and start planning my calendar around them. There are even nights, I'm slightly embarrassed to admit, when I go to bed excited for the breakfast I know I'll have in the morning. (It *is* the most important meal of the day, right?) Thinking too much about our next meal is somewhat humorous, but we can do the exact same type of overthinking when it comes to many areas of our lives. How many times have I sat in a beautiful moment and missed it completely because I was so wrapped up in what would come next? How often do I utter the phrase "I'm looking forward to…" when talking about my plans, while still in the midst of an already great day?

We can't be so caught up in what comes next that we miss what's here now. Be it for excitement (planning that next vacation or meal) or dread (worrying about an upcoming doctor's visit or exam), always looking ahead will cause us to live lives that never reach fullness. True fullness of life can only be reached when we are fully present in each and every moment.

Today's Scripture: **"Therefore do not worry about tomorrow, for tomorrow will worry about itself. Each day has enough trouble of its own" (Matthew 6:34 NIV).**

Today's Prayer: *Lord, forgive me for focusing too much on what's to come. I know that You have a plan for me today, and I want to do my best to be present in this moment. May I always remember to look for You in what is right in front of me. I don't want to miss You because my eyes are on the future while You're right here in my present. Amen.*

Day 21:
INSECURE CHOICES

I'll never forget the kick to my stomach when I discovered that my son Joey was being asked to do the homework of one of his supposed best friends. I found out accidentally. This other boy had been asking Joey to give him answers for questions he didn't understand. He told Joey that this was something good friends do. He told Joey that if he didn't give him the answers, he wasn't a real friend and the boy would find other true friends.

...sometimes doing the right thing can be a little lonely.

I was crushed. My sweet boy is sensitive and loyal and had been giving answers thinking he was being a good friend. I had to quickly sit him down and explain that this was in no way something a good friend did for another friend, and that his buddy was taking advantage of him. Joey cried and worried that he would lose the friendship and insisted it wasn't taking him too much time to do the other child's work. Oh, my heart hurts just thinking about it.

It's so easy for me to see the nonsense that Joey had bought into in this situation. He was being taken advantage of, plain and simple. If he was more secure about the friendship, he would have just said no without fear of any relational loss. But the other child was holding over Joey's head the threat that he would move on if Joey didn't do what he wanted.

The more I thought about it, the more I realized that I do the exact same thing at times. How often have I made decisions based on meeting the unrealistic expectations of others, too scared to say no for fear of being left behind or unaccepted? The answer, sadly, is too often to mention. It may be as simple as refusing to tell a group of ladies that I don't want to join them for a particular activity or meal, scared that if I do I'll be left out and passed by in the future. It could also, however, be as serious as a moral compromise to laugh at something I know is hurtful or offensive because I want to be considered hip or in.

What I explained to Joey is that sometimes doing the right thing can be a little lonely. And that's OK. God is with us, and pleasing Him is so much more important than any earthly approval or friendship. It's hard. So hard, in fact, that I am as guilty as Joey is at times of doing the things I know I shouldn't just for fear of reaction or reception. Today, we can't let fear, any fear, keep us from doing what we know to be right. We have to decide that no matter the cost we will keep integrity as our priority. If it hurts, let's hurt together! Ultimately, we can rejoice knowing that God is honored by our actions.

Today's Scripture: **"But you are not like that, for you are a chosen people. You are royal priests, a holy nation, God's very own possession. As a result, you can show others the goodness of God, for he called you out of the darkness into his wonderful light" (1 Peter 2:9 NLT).**

Today's Prayer: *Lord, help me to do right even when I'm afraid of what it will cost me. Nothing in my life is so important that I would chose it over You. Forgive me for times of compromise. Even if I feel alone, I know that You are with me. You are more than enough. Amen.*

Day 22:
LOSING? OR SO CLOSE TO WINNING?

School field days can be great fun. At their best, they are a time when children and parents can let loose and bond with laughter over the course of physical activities. The quintessential field day photos would surely include joyous-looking parents and children with their legs tied together, humorously hurdling over a finish line in victory. What these photos do not show, however, is the parent with a twisted ankle or a child throwing a tantrum over the lack of a blue ribbon.

My first field day experience was simultaneously my last. I was 6 years old and somehow assumed I'd be amazing at egg toss. For weeks, my dad and I practiced at home until we were sure we were unbeatable. When the day finally came, we proudly lined up wearing garbage bag dresses, and threw that very first toss — which also wound up being our last. Yes, I dropped the egg on the first toss. I was devastated.

When similar school events started rolling around for my kids, I was understandably hesitant. How could I let them face the distress that I had? I sucked it up, though, and allowed them to participate. What followed, shocked me and taught me a whole lot. Gavin was signed up for a particular competition. When he began competing, I noticed right away that this was not going to end in a victory. I gritted my teeth and prepared my "We're all winners!" speech.

But I never had to use it.

The race ended, and Gavin lost. But instead of running over to me in tears, he looked up at me with a huge smile and said, "I was SO close to winning!"

I was floored. How could he view it that way? My competitive and often polarizing nature makes it hard for me to see losses as anything other than what they are — losses. But this young boy was looking at the same situation I had repeatedly faced and giving me a completely new view on how to accept them.

Losses are not always just losses. Sometimes, you're very close to winning. Losses can also be celebrated. Sometimes you're only one more loss away from that ultimate win. Sometimes there's a lesson in the loss that will bring you far greater benefit than any win ever could. Sometimes the loss is part of the plan that will shape you into your best self.

Today's Scripture: **"In all this you greatly rejoice, though now for a little while you may have had to suffer grief in all kinds of trials. These have come so that the proven genuineness of your faith — of greater worth than gold, which perishes even though refined by fire — may result in praise, glory and honor when Jesus Christ is revealed"** **(1 Peter 1:6–7 NIV).**

Today's Prayer: *Lord, help my perspective today. I may have lost, but help me to see all I've gained. When I don't get what I think I want or need, show me where You are in that. I know You are always speaking, so I want to open my mind to hear from You in new ways. Amen.*

Day 23:
DON'T TRY TO BE THE PARENT!

Being a mom is 50 percent love, joy and heart-melting moments, and 50 percent repeating the same things over and over daily until you truly start to question your own sanity.

There are 47,586 (and counting!) amazing things about my oldest son, Joey. He is the most kind, thoughtful, hardworking boy, and I love him to bits. With his firstborn nature, however, has come a trait that I've often had to correct.

"Ella, if you don't stop doing that right now, you'll get in trouble!"

"Gavin, you're not brushing your teeth for long enough!"

Joey, for all his beautiful strengths, can often overextend his reach of authority and try to parent his brother and sister. I can't say that it's not nice to sometimes have an additional helping voice in the house when the younger two are doing things they shouldn't. The problem, though, is that his correction almost never goes over well. His brother and sister recognize the simple truth: Joey is not their parent. As such, they only push back more, and we wind up with two disobedient children and one ultra-frustrated older brother.

> *My role is only to let God be God and to be His child.*

Joey is not a parent. That's not his role. He is simply the older brother. He was not designed to discipline or correct his siblings. He flourishes with them the most when he just joins in with them in their games and acts as no more than their equal. He does not have my reach of authority because he does not have my life experience or position. He's a child and needs to be a child.

I'm so much like Joey sometimes. The only difference is that instead of playing the parent, I play God. How unequivocally dumb to believe that I could ever control my life? That is not my role. My role is only to let God be God and to be His child. Guess what? That is so much more than enough if I will simply allow it.

Maybe we all need a good, strong reminder that God is GOD. He is so big and all-knowing. He sees what we can't see and knows what we can't know. When we try to control our lives, we do it on a limited basis of knowledge. We were not made for the role of God in our lives. Like Joey trying to parent, if we attempt to be God, we'll surely fail. Let's let God be God. He is so much better at His job than we ever could hope to be!

Today's Scripture: **"When I consider your heavens, the work of your fingers, the moon and the stars, which you have set in place, what is mankind that you are mindful of them, human beings that you care for them?" (Psalm 8:3–4 NIV).**

Today's Prayer: *Thank You, Lord, that You are God and I am not! I repent from ever trying to be more than just Your child. I acknowledge Your role as the Lord of my life, and I will always try to submit to that order. When I forget, thank You for grace as I realize how poor a job I do of being in charge. Amen.*

Day 24:
HEAVEN ON MY MIND

It was hard to see our children face death for the first time. It happened when Jason's beloved Meemaw passed away one hot August day in 2017. We sat the boys down and explained to them that she had died, but that she was with Jesus now. The boys were unusually quiet, seemingly contemplative.

After a few moments, Joey spoke quietly, his voice filled with awe: "She's with Jesus right now!"

I got a chill down my spine. For all we do to avoid death and fear its impending arrival, I had forgotten the sweet joy that comes from knowing that when we die, we get to be with Jesus. Jesus. My Jesus. The One who has loved me from the start. He has carried me and held me and healed me. My God. My best friend. Jesus!

Has it been a long time since you've viewed death as anything other than the worst possible thing ever? Many of us, if we're honest, will admit that fear of death is one of our greatest fears. That's normal. We are finite. In this lifetime, all we know is this lifetime. We get so caught up in the things of this world that we panic when faced with the idea of no longer being here.

For believers, though, not being here means we are there. Where is there? Heaven! Life with Jesus in His perfect world where there is no more fear, death or sickness. Hallelujah!

It took a child's simple awe and understanding of the ultimate reality to remind me just how little I need to fear loss of this life. Making it to heaven is our goal. Heaven is our true home. I believe when we arrive in heaven, we will finally feel we are in the place we were meant to be—the place where we truly belong.

Let's let Joey's sweet, pure excitement for eternity urge us all to have an excitement for the life to come. Not only that, but let's let the truth of eternity with Jesus keep us from getting too worried or caught up in this life. It's not the end for us, friends, it's only the beginning!

Today's Scripture: **"We are confident, I say, and willing rather to be absent from the body, and to be present with the Lord" (2 Corinthians 5:8 KJV).**

Today's Prayer: *Lord, this world is not my home. I look forward to the day that I can spend eternity in heaven with You! Help me to always live with eternity in mind. When I'm upset, may I see just how little and insignificant these things really are. I want to live my life with full confidence in the home to come. Amen.*

Day 25:
THE PUPPY EYES GET ME EVERY TIME

Part of Gavin's "I'm the middle kid" schtick is a super-secret weapon he likes to call the "puppy eyes." The puppy eyes are basically an elongating of his already-large eyes, the folding down of his bottom lip, and some version of a pathetic whimper. He likes to pull this move out particularly when we are asking him to do something that he'd rather not do—go to bed, do homework, stop assaulting his sister, etc.

I can't stay mad when I look at Gavin's puppy eyes. Not because of the gesture itself, but because when I look at him, I am reminded of the awesome, creative, loving child he is. I am overwhelmed with my feelings of love for him. I know he's a stinker who is totally manipulating me with those darn puppy eyes, but hey, what can I say? The puppy eyes get me every time!

He loves me just because I'm His child.

God sees us like this. When He looks at us, it's with love. We are so quick to think that He sees our sins and shame and mistakes. That's us, though. We are the ones who tend to judge based on actions. God judges us based on only one action—the death of His Son on the cross for our sins. That one action was enough to see you as a forgiven, dearly loved child for the rest of your life!

I always struggle with the truth of God's love. I know He loves me, but since my mind bends so much toward logic and things that are bought and earned, I have a difficult time grasping the concept that someone who is perfect would love me regardless of my actions. But it's so amazing and so real. God does love me! He loves me just because I'm His child. He looks at me and can't resist my smile. How incredible is that?

Maybe today we all need to stop thinking of God as the angry judge who is sitting ready to zap us when we mess up. Maybe today we need to take a look at our own kids, realize our great love for them, and smile in the knowledge that our love is only a fraction of the love He feels for us. Wow. Sit with that for a moment. Or maybe more than a moment. Let's let it sink in. He loves us. He really loves us.

Today's Scripture**: "Therefore, as God's chosen people, holy and dearly loved, clothe yourselves with compassion, kindness, humility, gentleness and patience" (Colossians 3:12 NIV).**

Today's Prayer: *Lord, Your love is amazing. I know what I feel when I look at my children. Help me to remember that You see me that same way! I thank You for Your Father's heart toward me. You are gracious and loving, and I am so grateful to be Your child! Amen.*

Day 26:
YOU MAKE ME BRAVE

The dreaded day had finally arrived. All summer long I knew it was coming. I had a silent mental countdown that my body would revolt against as each day drew nearer. Finally, though, I could no longer delay the inevitable: My baby was starting preschool.

Ella is our youngest child and our only daughter. She is our rainbow baby after my previous pregnancy ended in a stillbirth. Knowing how fast time goes by because of the boys before her, we truly cherished each moment of our time with her as a baby and toddler.

When Ella turned 3, we decided to start her in a very part-time preschool program. She excitedly picked out a backpack and lunch box and learned her teacher's name. We went shopping for new shoes and school clothes and picked out the perfect first-day outfit.

When the first day of school arrived, she proudly held my hand and Jason's hand and walked boldly into her school. We arrived at her class, found her cubby, and sorted out her bag. Almost immediately, she took off, our hands dropped and forgotten. She headed straight to the play area and began attacking the mini kitchen. Jason and I looked on as her teacher redirected her to the proper first station (puzzles) and were amazed as she followed in compliance.

When the time came for Jason and me to leave, Ella simply looked up briefly from her puzzle and blew us a kiss. She was bold. She was brave. She was fearless. She wasn't bothered at all. Jason and I were both fighting back tears, but she was in the zone—dominating puzzles and well on her way to dominating the classroom. It was one of the most inspiring things I've ever seen.

I walked away from Ella's brightly decorated classroom feeling convicted about my own life. I will all too often allow fear to be the deciding factor in my decisions. I have let anxiety keep me from doing things I know I'd probably love or excel in. I've let worry make me do things that I know are illogical and senseless.

Looking at my daughter, I want to be as bold as she is. I don't want to shyly tiptoe into new experiences. I want to run in, full speed, eager to explore and achieve. I want to drop the hands of my security zones and soar into greatness.

Today, maybe we all need to remember what life was like before we knew about all the "what ifs." Ella doesn't sit in her room at night and think about all that can go wrong. She simply anticipates great day after great day. Yes, pain will come, but she's not going to let that stop her from going back to excited anticipation. And really, why should we? Let's jump into life today — brave! — and watch as our fearlessness opens new and exciting doors for us along the way!

Today's Scripture: **"Have I not commanded you? Be strong and courageous. Do not be afraid; do not be discouraged, for the LORD your God will be with you wherever you go" (Joshua 1:9 NIV).**

Today's Prayer: *Lord, make me bold and brave to be all You want me to be. I am tired of living life afraid. I want to take up the boldness of my children and go forward in all I do in You. Thank You for going with me so I don't have to be alone today. Amen.*

Day 27:
STEP-BY-STEP

Since Ella could walk, she has been obsessed with shoes. But not just any shoes. She's obsessed with *my* shoes. I am simultaneously incredibly proud and incredibly frustrated by this obsession. Many are the occasions in which I've walked into my closet only to find my shoe collection haphazardly thrown around. I know the culprit even before I walk into her room and find her delightfully dancing in a pair of my highest heels.

> *Everyone learns and grows at different paces, and our approach to that growth is key to our value as people.*

Ella has been an old soul from the moment she was born. Because of her verbal and emotional advancement, there are times that I forget just how young she really is. She loves to run in a pack with her older brothers and has been holding her own in a conversation with any adult since the time she was 3.

One night, though, while we walked up the stairs, hand in hand, I was reminded of just how little she actually was. I noticed that for each one of my steps, Ella was having to take two. It was kind of adorable really, watching her little legs work so hard to do something I barely gave notice to. Ella may have liked to walk in my heels, but she wasn't really able to take the steps that I was yet.

Do you get easily frustrated with those around you? Are you impatient? Maybe you need a reminder that no one else is in your same shoes and no one else has your exact perspective. You may think that people should know what you know or be able to do what you do, but the truth is that they simply don't.

Not everyone is where you are. Don't take for granted that people know what you know. Be patient. Take time to teach others. Take time to talk to others. We need to remember this in order to keep our compassion intact. It's easy to get frustrated with others, but we'll be a lot less frustrated if we stop and remember that we were where they are now not that long ago.

Whether it's someone we work with, a family member, or our own kids, it's not fair for us to deem that they should know more than they do. Everyone learns and grows at different paces, and our approach to that growth is key to our value as people. If we treat others with patience while they grow, they are far more likely to respond. If we get frustrated and angry at someone for not knowing what we know, while simultaneously not slowing down to show them, we have no one to blame but ourselves.

Let's pause and look around today. Maybe someone is struggling to keep up with us. If we selfishly forge ahead unaware, we'll lose them. Let's help others catch up. They're worth waiting for.

Today's Scripture: **"Preach the word; be prepared in season and out of season; correct, rebuke and encourage — with great patience and careful instruction" (2 Timothy 4:2 NIV).**

Today's Prayer: *Lord, forgive me for my impatience with others. How can I forget how patient You are with me? Help me today to pause and take notice of those who need some extra help and care. I never want to lose sight of where I've been while looking forward to where I'm going. Amen.*

Day 28:
LIMITS

Florida is hot. I mean, hot hot. Like standing on the face of the sun and turning the heat up on the thermostat hot. Here in Florida, our kids go back to school in early August, at the very peak of hotness. Because of this, I am constantly telling my kids, "DRINK MORE WATER!" and "DON'T FORGET SUNSCREEN!"

One day when I picked up my boys from school, I noticed that they were looking extra red in the face. After some inquiries, I found out that they'd ended the school day with an outdoors assembly. For well over an hour, they had been sitting in the sun at the peak of the heat of the day. I didn't think much of it until the fighting started.

Both boys began snapping at each other, eager to get in as many jabs (physical and verbal) as possible. Then, as we came home to do schoolwork, one boy spontaneously burst into tears and exclaimed that he just couldn't do any more work today. Later, at dinner, the other boy took up the tears his brother had started and bemoaned his "super mean" teacher (whom he had previously never complained about, of course).

I looked at my husband and told him that these kids were super over-exhausted and needed to never again get burnt out — physically or emotionally.

Was it really the sun? Were they simply overtired? Whatever it was, they had reached their limit. Anything, even the smallest thing, was provoking them to above normal emotional responses. Bottom line? They had reached their limit.

Oh, how I relate to that. There are days when I can hear truly challenging news and face it like a boss. I'll smile, quote a Scripture verse, and say, "God is good!" Then, there are days when I realize I'm out of coffee creamer, and I curl up in a ball on top of my kitchen counter, moaning out, "WHY ME????" while my poor kids look on in confusion.

We all have limits that we are smart to recognize and respect. We want to give our best self to this life, and we can't do that if we push past the point of our boundaries. How do we do this? Recognize the warning signs: Are you irritable? Tired? Crying for no reason? You may need a time-out to reset. Stop before taking on emotionally taxing tasks. Reassess your approach to things in these times.

Maybe you have been going and giving at full speed, with little time to receive your own strength from the Lord each day. This can't be. It simply won't work. You will crack at some point. Jesus Himself had to go away *often* to be with His Father (Luke 5:15–16). Why would we think we can do it any better than Him?

Today's Scripture: **"Yet the news about him spread all the more, so that crowds of people came to hear him and to be healed of their sicknesses. But Jesus often withdrew to lonely places and prayed" (Luke 5:15–16 NIV).**

Today's Prayer: *Lord, help me to set limits for myself before I burn out. I don't want to find myself at the bottom of my sanity because I didn't heed the warnings of boundaries. Forgive me for believing I can do it all. I need You to give me wisdom and strength today. Amen.*

Day 29:
THAT'S SPECIAL TO ME!

Miss Ella is a force. She is strong and bold, and she knows how to use her God-given intelligence to make things happen in her favor. One such use of said intelligence happened one night at the expense of my poor nephew. Ella and her cousin Ben were playing with some cheap toys, when Ella yanked a Frisbee out of Ben's hands. When the adults in the room told Ella to be kind and share, she looked at them, clutched the Frisbee tighter to her chest, and moaned, "But this is very special to me!"

The Frisbee had been "purchased" with tickets from our local Chuck E. Cheese and had an estimated value of approximately three cents (if that). Yet Ella knew enough at 3 years old to realize that if she was going to retain this item, she needed to ascribe value to it and make a dramatic play to enforce that.

I'm kind of in awe of how her mind works, to be honest.

The truth was that Ella could care less about this Frisbee; she was simply being bratty and not wanting to share with her cousin. Believe me, we all had a good laugh about it. I had a moment to ponder the incident after, though, and realized that I can be a whole lot like Ella when it comes to not relenting things that really don't matter.

Maybe it's not material items, but how many times have I stubbornly clung to something that is virtually worthless because I simply don't want to let go? I can't stand to see someone else be blessed by the thing I consider "mine," so I hold on to it long past it's due. This may be a job position, a relationship, or a leadership role, but it always ends the same: I overstay in something that I need to step away from.

What things are truly special to me, and what things are simply things? There is a huge difference, and recognizing that difference is important. Many things will compete for my energy, effort and attention. But only a few of those things are actually worth my energy, effort or attention. I can't get hung up on the worthless things. Why? Because there are too many things that are worthy and do deserve my time.

Maybe it's time to let go.

Today, we need to take stock. Are we clinging to the worthless under delusions of importance? Maybe it's time to let go. Maybe it's time to fight for what's worth fighting for and relinquish the rest.

Today's Scripture: **"Be very careful, then, how you live — not as unwise but as wise, making the most of every opportunity, because the days are evil. Therefore do not be foolish, but understand what the Lord's will is"** **(Ephesians 5:15–17 NIV).**

Today's Prayer: *Lord, forgive me for clinging to things that don't matter. Open my eyes to see what is important and worth fighting for. I know that not everything deserves my effort. Help me to decipher what I should do with my time. I want to do Your will always. Amen.*

Day 30:
I'M BASICALLY A MAN NOW

This past year brought about a big event in our home—my eldest reached double-digit status and turned 10! It was so crazy realizing I've been mom-ing for more than a decade. One day, relatively soon after Joey turned 10, he was speaking to a girlfriend of mine, and I happened to catch his conversation.

"Yeah, so I'm basically a man now," he said with a grin. My eyes bulged, and my friend and I exchanged a look over his head.

At 10 he was now a man. Basically.

I had a good laugh about it later with my husband, but it was only funny because we realized that being 10 hardly makes one a man. With his limited perspective, though, Joey truly saw himself as fully grown. Guess it's time to start asking him to pay rent?

This may be funny, but I can be the same way! I can think I'm so mature or so advanced at something where my spirituality is concerned. "I'm basically a spiritual giant now," I may as well say. But all it takes is one bad day or scare and *boom!* Where did the big, spiritually mature woman of God go? She must be hiding behind the tiny and timid woman I see shaking in the mirror.

The reality is that being more Christlike is not about becoming more advanced, but rather, becoming more broken. To grow in our Christianity really just means we realize how much we need Jesus each day. Assuming we are incredibly mature as believers can be a misstep of pride, and we all know what happens to us when pride takes a hold, don't we?

We need to learn to humble ourselves. Maybe you've been serving God your whole life. Maybe you've done more Bible studies than anyone you know. Maybe you know scripture forward and backward. Or maybe you're a brand-new Christian, and you feel intimidated by the people I just mentioned. Guess what? I've got news for both of you. We all (yes, all) have nothing to boast about. We are all just sinners who have been saved by God's grace (grace, for the record, cannot be earned, no matter how great you are).

Today, let's remember that spiritual growth is amazing, but thinking we're so spiritually grown is not. The more we grow in Christ, the more we realize that we are simply servants, modeling the example Jesus set for us. We will never stop growing as long as we remain in Him!

Today's Scripture: **"May I never boast except in the cross of our Lord Jesus Christ, through which the world has been crucified to me, and I to the world" (Galatians 6:14 NIV).**

Today's Prayer: *Lord, forgive me for thinking too highly of myself. I know that to grow in You means to become more like You – and You were the servant of all. I want to be more like You today. I want to be humble and aware of my great need for You. Amen.*

Day 31:
I'M HAPPY WHEN YOU LAUGH

My son Joey has the absolute BEST laugh in the world! His laughter is one of the most free, pure things I have ever heard. When he laughs, his whole body takes part. It's pure, unmitigated joy, and it gives me life just hearing it.

Joey can also get super-duper stressed by school, friends, and life. When he's in a stressful time, the laughter goes away. He appears anxious, and you can see strain over his whole body. Often, he's stressing about trying to be the best, trying to meet our expectations, and trying to do well. But I miss the laughter.

When I think of how I look at Joey and hurt when he hurts or laugh when he laughs, I can't help but think of God and the way He sees me. He loves when I laugh. Yes, He does. Somewhere along the way, I forgot that. Somewhere along the way, I became really hard on myself because I figured God was a God of justice (and He is) and that, as such, He must want me to obey at all times or else.

He's pleased with you.

The truth, though, is that God does love when we obey Him. But I'm a parent, and if I hate watching my kids strive and stress, how much more must God hate watching His creations strive for something they can never achieve anyway? He loves to see us walk in freedom. He loves to hear us laugh.

Have we gotten so caught up in trying to be good that we forget to just laugh and let God delight over us? My son can stress so hard that he winds up with headaches and stomachaches. As a mom, that makes my heart ache. Doesn't he know that his performance is secondary to me? I want him to do good, but I want him to be happy and to laugh and to find all the beauty that this world can bring.

God, our Father, created this world for us! But we stress and strive and try to please Him. Guess what? He's pleased with you. Yes, today. Yes, just as you are. You are His creation! He doesn't just love you; He likes you too! Relax in His embrace and laugh. Just laugh. Smile, find joy, and then laugh some more. He loves it when you laugh.

Today's Scripture: **"For the LORD takes delight in his people" (Psalm 149:4a NIV).**

Today's Prayer: *Lord, thank You that You love me and like me just as I am. I ask forgiveness for trying to somehow be good enough for You. I know it's not about me, but about You and what Your Son did for me. Help me take time to just laugh today. My laugh came from You, and I give it back to You in joy. Amen.*

NOTES